AF605342

OUTBACK

First published in 2025 by New Holland Publishers
Sydney, Australia.
newhollandpublishers.com

 A record of this book is held at the National Library of Australia.

ISBN: 9781760797836

Managing Director: Fiona Schultz
General Manager/Publisher: Olga Dementiev
Designer: Andrew Davies
Production Director: Arlene Gippert
Printed in China

OUTBACK

SOUTHERN

LAST
PUB
FOR
386
KM.

8kph
KANGAROO
CROSSING

CREST

RAILWAY
CROSSING
STOP
LOOK
FOR
TRAINS
RAILWAY

CROSSING

HILL
BOOT HILL →

230

STAFF
ONLY
Gents

Ladies

OUTBACK

- At the centre of Australia's outback history are the **traditional owners** of the land, Aboriginal Australians.
- Aboriginal people have lived in the Outback for at least **50,000 years**.
- **Kalgoorlie**, Western Australia, is Australia's largest and possibly most famous outback city.
- Temperatures in the central deserts can reach as high as **50°C** (120°F) on summer days and drop below freezing to **–10°C** (15°F) during winter nights.
- The Outback is rich in **wildlife**; from red kangaroos to dingos, bird life is in abundance from cockatoos to galahs and there are many other animals like camels, pigs, foxes and wild goats.
- **Tourism** is a major industry across the Outback for Australians and international visitors with the most popular attractions such as Uluru, Devils Marbles, Kakadu National Park, Kata Tjuta (The Olgas) and experiencing beautiful colourful sunsets.
- The **Royal Flying Doctor Service** started in 1928 and helps people who live in the outback of Australia.

THE AUSTRALIAN STOCKMAN'S HALL OF FAME